T0401284

What
DO YOU THINK?

SHOULD WE PROTECT THE ENVIRONMENT?

BY RAYMIE DAVIS

Gareth Stevens
PUBLISHING

Please visit our website, www.garethstevens.com. For a free color catalog of all our high-quality books, call toll free 1-800-542-2595 or fax 1-877-542-2596.

Library of Congress Cataloging-in-Publication Data

Names: Davis, Raymie, author.
Title: Should we protect the environment? / by Raymie Davis.
Description: New York : Gareth Stevens Publishing, [2023] | Series: What do you think? | Includes index. | Audience: Grades 2-3
Identifiers: LCCN 2021044978 (print) | LCCN 2021044979 (ebook) | ISBN 9781538278796 (paperback) | ISBN 9781538278819 (library binding) | ISBN 9781538278802 (set) | ISBN 9781538278826 (ebook)
Subjects: LCSH: Environmental protection–Juvenile literature. | Environmentalism–Juvenile literature.
Classification: LCC TD170.15 .D39 2023 (print) | LCC TD170.15 (ebook) | DDC 363.7–dc23
LC record available at https://lccn.loc.gov/2021044978
LC ebook record available at https://lccn.loc.gov/2021044979

First Edition

Portions of this work were originally authored by David Anthony and published as *Is It Our Job to Protect the Environment?*. All new material this edition authored by Raymie Davis.

Published in 2023 by
Gareth Stevens Publishing
29 East 21st Street
New York, NY 10010

Editor: Caitie McAneney
Designer: Michael Flynn

Photo credits: Cover, p. 1 © D-Keine/iStock; back cover and series background MYMNY/Shutterstock.com; p. 4 Monkey Business Images/Shutterstock.com; p. 5 Pixel-Shot/Shutterstock.com; p. 6 My Photo Buddy/Shutterstock.com; p. 7 BLACKWHITEPAILYN/Shutterstock.com; p. 9 Foto 4440/Shutterstock.com; p. 11 MIND AND I/Shutterstock.com; p. 13 Magnifical Productions/Shutterstock.com; p. 15 Amit kg/Shutterstock.com; p. 16 StockMediaSeller/Shutterstock.com; p. 17 Andy Dean Photography/Shutterstock.com; p. 19 Nina Buday/Shutterstock.com; p. 21 Halfpoint/Shutterstock.com.

Printed in the United States of America

Some of the images in this book illustrate individuals who are models. The depictions do not imply actual situations or events.

CPSIA compliance information: Batch #CSGS23: For further information contact Gareth Stevens, New York, New York at 1-800-542-2595.

Find us on

CONTENTS

WORDS IN THE GLOSSARY APPEAR IN **BOLD** TYPE THE FIRST TIME THEY ARE USED IN THE TEXT.

HARMING AND HELPING

Our **environment** is key to our **survival** on Earth. Without clean air, water, and land, we wouldn't be able to live here. People harm the environment when they pollute the air or water or cut down trees. They help the environment when they work to protect it, or keep it safe.

Some people believe they shouldn't have to protect the planet. Others believe it's our job to protect the environment and fix problems that we've caused.

DO YOU THINK WE SHOULD HELP THE ENVIRONMENT? LEARNING BOTH SIDES OF THE **DEBATE** CAN HELP YOU MAKE AN OPINION.

WHAT IS CLIMATE CHANGE?

Climate change is a big issue with the environment. Climate is the weather in a place over a long period of time. Gases put into the air by people are causing the planet to get warmer. This affects weather around the world.

As Earth gets warmer, **polar ice** melts, which puts more water in the oceans. This can cause flooding. Climate change also leads to wildfires, strong storms, and dry spells. This harms **habitats** for animals. It forces people from their homes.

Think ABOUT IT !

AS OF 2020, THE YEARS 2016 AND 2020 WERE TWO OF THE HOTTEST EVER RECORDED.

HIGH TEMPERATURES FROM **GLOBAL** WARMING MAKE SOME PLACES HARD TO LIVE IN.

NOTHING BUT NORMAL

Some people think that climate change is normal. They aren't worried about global warming. They argue that Earth has gone through periods of climate change many times before.

At different times in Earth's history, much of the planet was covered with ice. After an ice age, the planet would go through a period of warming. People don't think there's any reason to try to stop what they see as part of a natural cycle of warming and cooling. They argue that **glaciers** melting is normal.

SCIENTISTS STUDY GLACIERS AND HOW THEY ARE MELTING TO LEARN MORE ABOUT THE PAST AND PRESENT OF CLIMATE CHANGE.

9

OUR FAULT

Some people say that we have to protect the environment because issues like climate change are our fault. Most scientists believe the planet is warming so quickly because of human activity. Greenhouse gases are gases people put into the air through burning **fossil fuels**. They trap the sun's warmth on Earth, which makes the planet hotter.

Because people are the main cause of the problem, many believe people should also try to fix it. They want to reduce greenhouse gases and pollution.

Think ABOUT IT!

GREENHOUSE GASES ARE OFTEN PUT INTO THE AIR BY BURNING COAL AND OIL FOR POWER.

GREENHOUSE GASES

CARBON DIOXIDE
FROM OIL AND COAL

METHANE
FROM CATTLE AND FERTILIZER

NITROUS OXIDE
FROM GASOLINE AND FARMING

TREES TAKE IN SOME GREENHOUSE GASES THAT HARM THE PLANET. SOME PEOPLE BELIEVE WE SHOULD STOP CUTTING DOWN TREES AND PLANT NEW ONES.

11

HIGH COSTS

Some people think the cost of protecting the environment is too high. Changes to cars and factories that give off fewer greenhouse gases can cost a lot of money. Some people feel people and businesses shouldn't have to spend that money.

In some cases, people also worry that taking care of the environment could become more important than making sure people have jobs. Jobs in the fossil fuels business, such as coal mining, are important to the workers who need them.

SOME PEOPLE THINK PROTECTING THE ENVIRONMENT SHOULDN'T BE MORE IMPORTANT THAN PROTECTING PEOPLE'S JOBS.

STAYING HEALTHY

Some people argue that our health depends on the health of the environment. We should work to keep the planet healthy because that keeps people healthy. Clean air and water are good for all living things.

Studies have shown that pollution can make people very sick. Dirty water causes many different diseases, or illnesses. Air pollution can lead to heart disease and lung **cancer**. It can also cause babies to not grow normally. Air pollution is often worse in places with many people and factories.

SMOG IS A COMBINATION OF HARMFUL SMOKE AND FOG. IT IS A PROBLEM IN PLACES WITH MANY FACTORIES AND PEOPLE, LIKE NEW DELHI, INDIA.

PERSONAL FREEDOM

Many people want to protect the environment in some way. However, they feel they should have the personal freedom to decide how to live.

Today, many governments want to pass laws to reduce pollution and keep animals and plants safe. However, there are people who don't like these laws. They think the government shouldn't tell them what to do. They believe their personal freedoms are more important than the environment. They don't want governments to change the way they live.

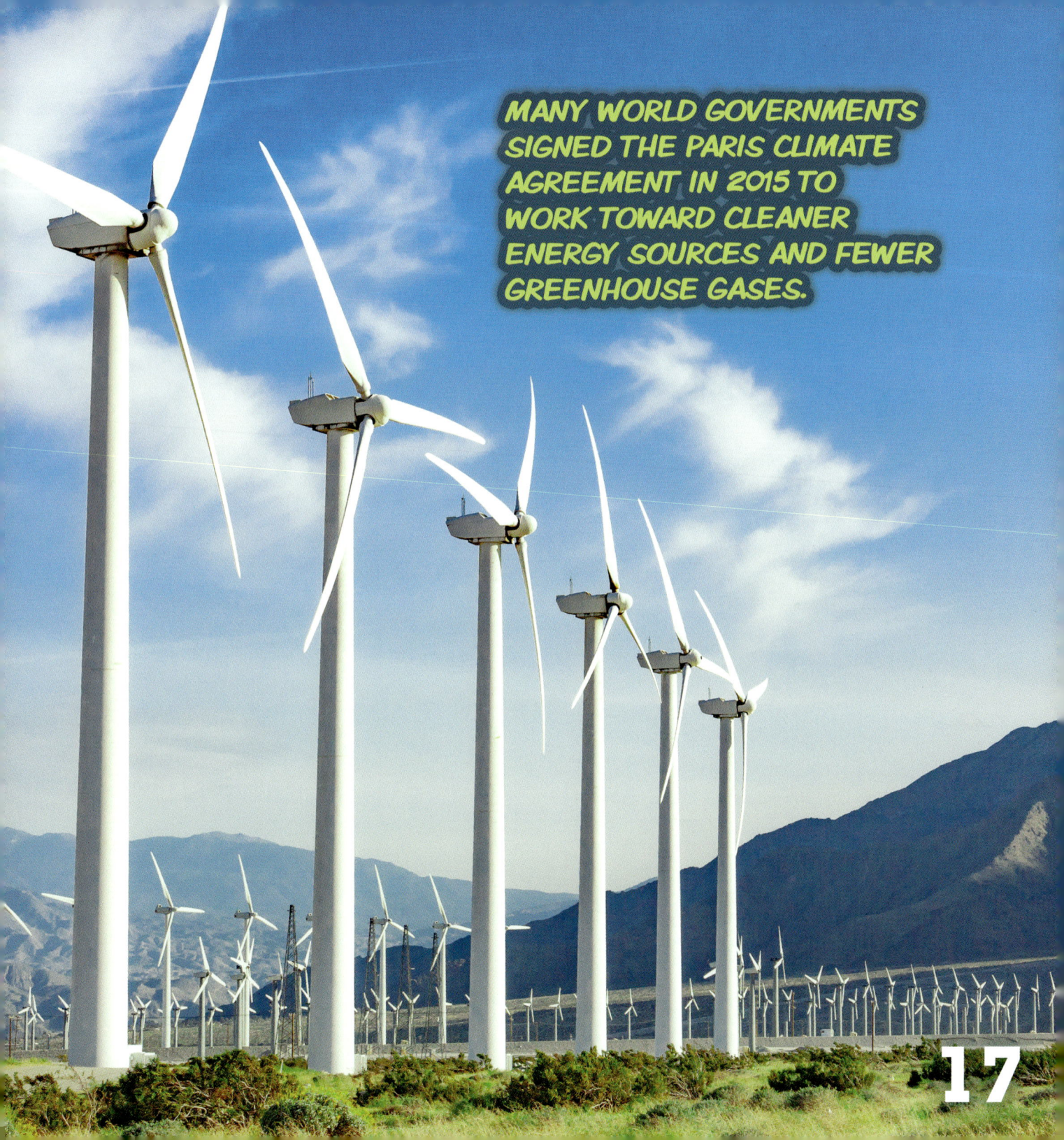

MANY WORLD GOVERNMENTS SIGNED THE PARIS CLIMATE AGREEMENT IN 2015 TO WORK TOWARD CLEANER ENERGY SOURCES AND FEWER GREENHOUSE GASES.

17

KEEPING IT CLEAN

Climate change isn't only an issue for our time. It's something that will affect people for hundreds of years to come. Many people want to leave a clean and healthy planet for their children and future people.

There's only one Earth. This is why many people believe it's so important to take care of it. They argue that there's no Planet B, or another place for humans to live. Earth provides all of our resources, and keeping it clean benefits everyone. Humankind depends on it.

MORE THAN 4 MILLION PEOPLE TOOK PART IN CLIMATE **PROTESTS** WORLDWIDE IN SEPTEMBER 2019. INCLUDING MANY CHILDREN.

THERE ARE MANY WAYS TO HELP THE ENVIRONMENT, FROM PLANTING TREES TO EATING LOCAL FOODS.

THE CLIMATE DEBATE

The climate debate is a heated one. It's also fairly new to humans. Until recent decades, people didn't understand how much they could affect the environment. Now, though, scientists have shown us how much our actions can help and hurt the planet we call home.

Many people think we need to protect the environment. However, other people think it's not our job, and that life as they know it is more important. Where do you stand?

MANY PEOPLE HAVE MARCHED FOR CLIMATE CHANGE ISSUES IN HOPES OF HELPING THE PLANET.

21

GLOSSARY

cancer: a sometimes deadly sickness in which cells grow in the body in ways they should not

debate: an argument or discussion about an issue, generally between two sides

economy: the money made in an area and how it is made

environment: the natural world in which a plant or animal lives

fertilizer: something added to the soil to help plants grow

fossil fuel: a fuel, such as coal, oil, or natural gas, that is formed in the earth from dead plants or animals

glacier: a large body of ice

global: relating to the whole world

habitat: the natural place where an animal or plant lives

polar ice: sheets of ice found at the North Pole and South Pole

protest: an event at which a group objects to an idea, an act, or a way of doing something

survival: the state of continuing to live

FOR MORE INFORMATION

BOOKS

Bergin, Raymond. *Terrible Storms*. Minneapolis, MN: Bearport Publishing, 2022.

French, Jess. *What a Waste: Rubbish, Recycling, and Protecting Our Planet*. London, UK: DK Children, 2019.

Scibilia, Jade Zora. *Climate Change*. New York, NY: PowerKids Press, 2019.

WEBSITES

Climate Facts for Kids
www.fredonia.edu/about/offices/climate-education-initiative/climate-facts-kids
Learn more about climate and why it's changing around the world.

National Geographic Kids: Climate Change
kids.nationalgeographic.com/science/article/climate-change
Discover how climate change affects people and animals—and what you can do about it.

What's Climate Change? And What Can I Do?
www.climaterealityproject.org/blog/just-kids-what-climate-change-and-what-can-i-do
What can kids do to help climate change? Read this resource to find out.

INDEX